Network Marketing 90 Day Blitz Planner

2016-2018

This Planner Belongs to:

_____

_____

_____

Network Marketing 90 Day Blitz Planner

First Edition: December 2016
Printed in the United States of America
ISBN-13: 978-0-9969314-9-6
Published by OmediO Corp

Made for Network Marketers
by Network Marketers

This planner has been customized exclusively for Network Marketers. Every page has been thought out carefully with your success in mind. Whether you are just starting out or have been in the business for a while, a 90 Day Blitz in your business could be the difference between buying the pay-per-view for this years' Superbowl or flying your friends and family out to see the game in person!

Our Daily Method of Operation will ensure you stay on track towards your goals and to keep personal accountability within your business as well as keeping accountable to anyone in your upline or downline that is also using this planner.

Whether your goal is to make some additional income, earn a specific company bonus, qualify for your company's exotic vacations, or become the top producer in your company, this planner will help organize you which in turn will help in making your dreams a reality.

We can say with amazing certainty that every successful Network Marketer has a system to keep their goals and milestones planned out so they can maximize their success. We researched the daily activities of millionaire earners in the network marketing industry and created this planner with that knowledge.

Enjoy!

- 90 Day Blitz Planner team

Table of Contents

People often ask why we say that network marketing is a better way of making money than a traditional job or business. Network marketing leaders come from all walks of life and we have a simple explanation on why they believe that the industry is the best vehicle out there for the average person to create a better lifestyle for themselves and their families. The following three examples will illustrate the three basic vehicles there are to make money in a simple way to help you remember.

THE BICYCLE: A JOB

This is the most common vehicle people use to get to where they want to go. The reason a bicycle is appealing is primarily because of it's comfort level. Bicycles are easy to get and if you lose one, it won't be that hard to find another  one. Once you get the hang of riding a bike, you don't need too much thought to keep it going and most people ride bikes, especially since there is little to no cost financially to own. The problem with bicycles is that it'll take you forever to get to where you want to go. Imagine if you have "take a vacation to Cabo San Lucas" on your dream board. Now imagine how long it will take you to get there on a bicycle. Imagine how long it will take you to reach your dreams with a typical job. Most people are on the 40/40 program where they will work 40 hours a week for 40 years and hope they can retire with enough money to sustain themselves, let alone take those awesome vacations they've been dreaming about. Although there may not be much financial cost to owning a bicycle, the real price is how much of your time will go into this vehicle without a guarantee of getting to your destination.

THE CAR: TRADITIONAL BUSINESS, REAL ESTATE, ETC.

Sometimes, people realize that the bicycle is too slow or they realize that it will never allow them to reach their destination within their lifetime. Many of those people trade in their bicycle for a nice car. The car is super appealing because it has the potential to go much faster than a bicycle. Just the thought of reaching your destination much faster is very exciting, what could be the downside? Depending on what car you can afford, it could be an unpredictable vehicle. It may run great in the summer but terrible in the winter. Just like a car, in a traditional business, your business may run great when there is a great economy and people are spending money or when you're working your business 16 hours per day... But what do you do in the winter (bad economy)? Your vehicle may stop working completely. It can completely drain your time and cause you to lose lots of your own money to keep it going AND to pay your bills. Even though having a car has the potential to have you reach your destination much faster than a bicycle, there are so many things outside of your control that can destroy your vehicle. When this happens, most people feel like they have no choice and go back to riding that bicycle and start from scratch heading toward their destination.

THE LEASED JET: NETWORK MARKETING

The jet is the fastest of all the vehicles the average person can choose to reach their destination. You can imagine any destination in the world. There is nothing out of reach of the jet AND it will get you there FAST... once you learn how to fly. There are four things people need to understand so they know that they are flying in a jet:

Why Network Marketing?

1. Residual Income
- The ability to do the work once and get paid over and over and over.

2. Leverage
- Building a team to get paid on the efforts of others versus just your own.

3. Proven System
- The team has built a system with a high success rate versus a high failure rate if you try to figure it out on your own.

4. Mentor
- Having someone who has mastered the system that is willing to teach you step by step and knows any issues you may go through and can guide you through them.

When you have these four things understood, you have a jet. You have all the benefits of having a jet without the millions of dollars that go into buying it. Your company already spent the money developing a solid product/service and compensation plan. Your leaders have already spent years developing a solid system that is duplicatable. But with the power of being able to get to their destination in a jet, why don't more people take advantage of it? Well, because you have to get a pilot's license. Unlike the bicycle and sometimes the car, there are skills that have to be learned and mastered before you can fly the jet to your dreams. These skills take time to acquire and you have to remain coachable every step of the way. The best thing about a system is that it teaches you to get your pilot's license. It shows you what buttons you push, what levers to pull, and what to say to your crew... just be coachable and you'll have your license in no time. Then you'll be able to get to where you want to go utilizing the fastest vehicle possible.

Setting and Achieving Goals

Decide on a goal

1. Be specific

2. Be realistic

3. Always write down the goal

4. Never say "I want to." Instead say, "I will"
This puts your goal in your mind as non-negotiable, it's gonna happen.

Example: I will hit the first rank in my company.

Set a deadline for your goal

1. Set a specific date or time frame

2. Break down the goal into smaller goals

Example: I have to hit the first rank in my company in 31 days. The rank is X personal customers and Y distributors each with their own personal customers.

Create a plan

1. Create an overall action plan

2. Break the action plan down into basic steps and a daily plan.

Example: In order to do this, I have to expose 20 people to my business. The best way to do this is to have a few home meetings. I also have to call at least 2 people a day using the scripts in our documents to get my customers.

Find an accountability partner

1. Tell everyone your goal

2. Have a partner hold you to your commitment.

Example: Hey babe, I have get my customers and distributors but to do that I need to make my calls and have my home meetings. Can you be there during everything to make sure I get it done?

Daily Method of Operation (DMO)

Productive work versus busy work

Each day in this planner will have a Daily Method of Operation (DMO) scoreboard designed to help you focus on activities that keep you productive rather than keep you busy.

Weekly Goals
Part Time · 20 points per week
Full Time · 50 points per week

Points

1   *Pique Interest* - This is simply finding out if someone is interested in your business. You can talk to people, give out your business card, send someone a link, have them download your app, or send them to a website.

1   *Successful 3way Call* - If someone wants to know more after you connect them with your upline or they agree to come to a presentation, you get points. Only award yourself these points if the call is successful.

2   *Presentation (1 or 2 guests)* - Show the opportunity through some type of presentation (2on1, phone 1thru9, home meeting, etc) where there are 1 or 2 prospects.

3   *Presentation (3+ guests)* - Show the opportunity through some type of presentation (2on1, phone 1thru9, home meeting, etc) where there are 3+ prospects.

5   *Presentation (5+ guests)* - Show the opportunity through some type of presentation (2on1, phone 1thru9, home meeting, etc) where there are 3+ prospects.

10   *Presentation (10+ guests)* - Show the opportunity through some type of presentation (2on1, phone 1thru9, home meeting, etc) where there are 3+ prospects.

3   *Distributor Acquisition* - Whenever someone signs up in your business.

2   *Customer Acquisition* - Whenever you get a new customer.

2   *Launch New Distributor* - Successfully launch a new distributor.

The 4 Personality Types

A communication tool

The best network marketers understand that you have to be able to communicate with the people you are presenting to. Your presentations will either attract or repel certain people depending on how they feel about you and how the information is presented. Network marketing is an attraction business and you need to know the 4 types of people you will always be presenting to. The sooner you can identify their personality types and relate to them, the better the chance you will have at influencing them and their decision.

Here are the 4 personality types:

SHARK

DOMINANT PERSONALITY, LEADER, BIG PICTURE PERSON, NATURAL CLOSER

EXAMPLE
Car sales people, door2door sales people, or anyone who is aggressive

WAY TO RELATE
Talk about money, the spotlight, or the recognition

STRENGTHS
Aggressive builder

WEAKNESS
Won't listen to you, hard-headed, competitive

URCHIN

DETAIL ORIENTED, SECURITY AND STABILITY, NEEDS TO KNOW EVERYTHING

EXAMPLE
Engineers, doctors, lawyers

WAY TO RELATE
Facts and figures. Be patient and take extra time to create value.

STRENGTHS
Brings credibility, will always do everything right

WEAKNESS
Too analytical, not as coachable, moves slow, majors in the minors

The 4 Personality Types

D O L P H I N

FUN, LIFE OF THE PARTY, VERY LIKEABLE, LOTS OF FRIENDS, LIMITED ATTENTION SPAN

EXAMPLE
Club promoters, event planners, socialites

WAY TO RELATE
Talk about how much fun they will have and the exciting aspects of your business (vacations)

STRENGTHS
Will bring a lot of people into the business

WEAKNESS
Hard time following through with anyone or anything

W H A L E

LOVES TO HELP OTHERS, CONCERNED ABOUT WHAT OTHERS THINK, MONEY IS NOT THE BIGGEST MOTIVATOR

EXAMPLE
Teachers, coaches, pastors, community leaders

WAY TO RELATE
Talk about helping people, making a difference, and supporting a cause

STRENGTHS
Quality relationships and a lot of trust within their circle

WEAKNESS
Very slow to take action, has a lot of fear and worry

THE WEEK

The following pages are the meat and potatoes of this planner. Here is where you will write down your accomplishments, things to improve on, and fill out your Daily Method of Operation (DMO). Going from Monday to Sunday, every week will begin with a page that looks like this:

REMEMBER: FULL TIME 50+ POINTS   PART TIME 20+ POINTS

Here you will recap the success of your goals and ways you can improve upon the following week. You will also tally up your points from the DMO to see where you are at. Starting from your second week, you will also see spaces to write down any upcoming holidays (refer to the Holidays and Observences section). Also, you will have spaces to write down what your goals are for this week. Here is an example:

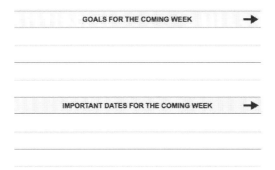

ALSO! If you are starting a brand new, 90 day blitz in your business, check off, color in, or put a sticker on the box at the top right box so you can remember when you decided to relaunch your business and go on a powerful 90 day run!

DAY BY DAY

This day by day guide will keep you focused and on target for whatever goals you have for this particular day, week, month, or even year. At the top you will write down the correct dates (refer to the end of the book for 2016-2018 calendars).

You will be able to fill in any appointments you have setup, keep on task with your Top Priorities for the day, any notes that you want to refer to later, and also your very important (pretty much required) DMO totals. Here's what this will look like:

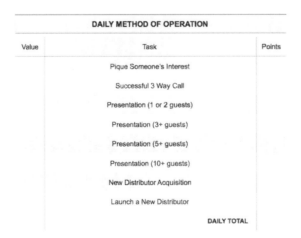

START YOUR 90 DAY BLITZ!

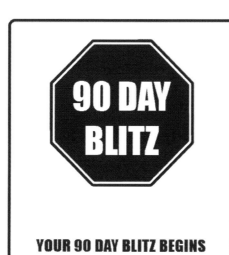

YOUR 90 DAY BLITZ BEGINS TODAY!

GOALS FOR THE COMING WEEK ➡

IMPORTANT DATES FOR THE COMING WEEK ➡

MONDAY

TODAY'S TOP PRIORITIES

DAILY METHOD OF OPERATION

Value	Task	Points
1	Pique Someone's Interest	
1	Successful 3 Way Call	
2	Presentation (1 or 2 guests)	
3	Presentation (3+ guests)	
5	Presentation (5+ guests)	
10	Presentation (10+ guests)	
3	New Distributor Acquisition	
2	New Customer Acquisition	
2	Launch a New Distributor	
	DAILY TOTAL	

DATE:

APPOINTMENTS

am/pm   am/pm

am/pm   am/pm

am/pm   am/pm

am/pm   am/pm

am/pm   am/pm

am/pm   am/pm

am/pm   am/pm

DAILY NOTES

TUESDAY

DAILY METHOD OF OPERATION

Value	Task	Points
1	Pique Someone's Interest	
1	Successful 3 Way Call	
2	Presentation (1 or 2 guests)	
3	Presentation (3+ guests)	
5	Presentation (5+ guests)	
10	Presentation (10+ guests)	
3	New Distributor Acquisition	
2	New Customer Acquisition	
2	Launch a New Distributor	
	DAILY TOTAL	

DATE:

APPOINTMENTS

_____ am/pm   _____ am/pm

_____ am/pm   _____ am/pm

_____ am/pm   _____ am/pm

_____ am/pm   _____ am/pm

_____ am/pm   _____ am/pm

_____ am/pm   _____ am/pm

_____ am/pm   _____ am/pm

DAILY NOTES

WEDNESDAY

TODAY'S TOP PRIORITIES

DAILY METHOD OF OPERATION

Value	Task	Points
1	Pique Someone's Interest	
1	Successful 3 Way Call	
2	Presentation (1 or 2 guests)	
3	Presentation (3+ guests)	
5	Presentation (5+ guests)	
10	Presentation (10+ guests)	
3	New Distributor Acquisition	
2	New Customer Acquisition	
2	Launch a New Distributor	
	DAILY TOTAL	

DATE:

APPOINTMENTS

am/pm

am/pm

am/pm

am/pm

am/pm

am/pm

am/pm

am/pm

am/pm

am/pm

am/pm

am/pm

am/pm

am/pm

DAILY NOTES

THURSDAY

TODAY'S TOP PRIORITIES

DAILY METHOD OF OPERATION

Value	Task	Points
1	Pique Someone's Interest	
1	Successful 3 Way Call	
2	Presentation (1 or 2 guests)	
3	Presentation (3+ guests)	
5	Presentation (5+ guests)	
10	Presentation (10+ guests)	
3	New Distributor Acquisition	
2	New Customer Acquisition	
2	Launch a New Distributor	
	DAILY TOTAL	

DATE:

APPOINTMENTS

am/pm

am/pm

am/pm

am/pm

am/pm

am/pm

am/pm

am/pm

am/pm

am/pm

am/pm

am/pm

am/pm

am/pm

DAILY NOTES

FRIDAY

TODAY'S TOP PRIORITIES

DAILY METHOD OF OPERATION

Value	Task	Points
1	Pique Someone's Interest	
1	Successful 3 Way Call	
2	Presentation (1 or 2 guests)	
3	Presentation (3+ guests)	
5	Presentation (5+ guests)	
10	Presentation (10+ guests)	
3	New Distributor Acquisition	
2	New Customer Acquisition	
2	Launch a New Distributor	
	DAILY TOTAL	

DATE:

APPOINTMENTS

am/pm   am/pm

am/pm   am/pm

am/pm   am/pm

am/pm   am/pm

am/pm   am/pm

am/pm   am/pm

am/pm   am/pm

DAILY NOTES

SATURDAY

DAILY METHOD OF OPERATION

Value	Task	Points
1	Pique Someone's Interest	
1	Successful 3 Way Call	
2	Presentation (1 or 2 guests)	
3	Presentation (3+ guests)	
5	Presentation (5+ guests)	
10	Presentation (10+ guests)	
3	New Distributor Acquisition	
2	New Customer Acquisition	
2	Launch a New Distributor	
	DAILY TOTAL	

DATE:

APPOINTMENTS

am/pm   am/pm

am/pm   am/pm

am/pm   am/pm

am/pm   am/pm

am/pm   am/pm

am/pm   am/pm

am/pm   am/pm

DAILY NOTES

SUNDAY

TODAY'S TOP PRIORITIES

DAILY METHOD OF OPERATION

Value	Task	Points
1	Pique Someone's Interest	
1	Successful 3 Way Call	
2	Presentation (1 or 2 guests)	
3	Presentation (3+ guests)	
5	Presentation (5+ guests)	
10	Presentation (10+ guests)	
3	New Distributor Acquisition	
2	New Customer Acquisition	
2	Launch a New Distributor	
	DAILY TOTAL	

DATE:

APPOINTMENTS

_____ am/pm _____   _____ am/pm _____

_____ am/pm _____   _____ am/pm _____

_____ am/pm _____   _____ am/pm _____

_____ am/pm _____   _____ am/pm _____

_____ am/pm _____   _____ am/pm _____

_____ am/pm _____   _____ am/pm _____

_____ am/pm _____   _____ am/pm _____

DAILY NOTES

RECAP YOUR PREVIOUS WEEK

AND

PREPARE FOR YOUR NEXT WEEK

REMEMBER:　　　FULL TIME 50+ POINTS　　　PART TIME 20+ POINTS

DAILY METHOD OF OPERATION TOTALS FOR THE WEEK

Value	Task	Points
1	Pique Someone's Interest	
1	Successful 3 Way Call	
2	Presentation (1 or 2 guests)	
3	Presentation (3+ guests)	
5	Presentation (5+ guests)	
10	Presentation (10+ guests)	
3	New Distributor Acquisition	
2	New Customer Acquisition	
2	Launch a New Distributor	
	WEEKLY TOTAL	

← TOP ACCOMPLISHMENTS FOR THIS PAST WEEK

← THINGS TO IMPROVE ON

GOALS FOR THE COMING WEEK →

IMPORTANT DATES FOR THE COMING WEEK →

MONDAY

DAILY METHOD OF OPERATION

Value	Task	Points
1	Pique Someone's Interest	
1	Successful 3 Way Call	
2	Presentation (1 or 2 guests)	
3	Presentation (3+ guests)	
5	Presentation (5+ guests)	
10	Presentation (10+ guests)	
3	New Distributor Acquisition	
2	New Customer Acquisition	
2	Launch a New Distributor	
	DAILY TOTAL	

DATE:

APPOINTMENTS

am/pm   am/pm

am/pm   am/pm

am/pm   am/pm

am/pm   am/pm

am/pm   am/pm

am/pm   am/pm

am/pm   am/pm

DAILY NOTES

TUESDAY

TODAY'S TOP PRIORITIES

DAILY METHOD OF OPERATION

Value	Task	Points
1	Pique Someone's Interest	
1	Successful 3 Way Call	
2	Presentation (1 or 2 guests)	
3	Presentation (3+ guests)	
5	Presentation (5+ guests)	
10	Presentation (10+ guests)	
3	New Distributor Acquisition	
2	New Customer Acquisition	
2	Launch a New Distributor	
	DAILY TOTAL	

DATE:

APPOINTMENTS

am/pm	am/pm
am/pm	am/pm
am/pm	am/pm
am/pm	am/pm
am/pm	am/pm
am/pm	am/pm
am/pm	am/pm

DAILY NOTES

WEDNESDAY

TODAY'S TOP PRIORITIES

DAILY METHOD OF OPERATION

Value	Task	Points
1	Pique Someone's Interest	
1	Successful 3 Way Call	
2	Presentation (1 or 2 guests)	
3	Presentation (3+ guests)	
5	Presentation (5+ guests)	
10	Presentation (10+ guests)	
3	New Distributor Acquisition	
2	New Customer Acquisition	
2	Launch a New Distributor	
	DAILY TOTAL	

DATE:

APPOINTMENTS

am/pm   am/pm

am/pm   am/pm

am/pm   am/pm

am/pm   am/pm

am/pm   am/pm

am/pm   am/pm

am/pm   am/pm

DAILY NOTES

THURSDAY

DAILY METHOD OF OPERATION

Value	Task	Points
1	Pique Someone's Interest	
1	Successful 3 Way Call	
2	Presentation (1 or 2 guests)	
3	Presentation (3+ guests)	
5	Presentation (5+ guests)	
10	Presentation (10+ guests)	
3	New Distributor Acquisition	
2	New Customer Acquisition	
2	Launch a New Distributor	
	DAILY TOTAL	

DATE:

APPOINTMENTS

am/pm

am/pm

am/pm

am/pm

am/pm

am/pm

am/pm

am/pm

am/pm

am/pm

am/pm

am/pm

am/pm

am/pm

DAILY NOTES

FRIDAY

TODAY'S TOP PRIORITIES

DAILY METHOD OF OPERATION

Value	Task	Points
1	Pique Someone's Interest	
1	Successful 3 Way Call	
2	Presentation (1 or 2 guests)	
3	Presentation (3+ guests)	
5	Presentation (5+ guests)	
10	Presentation (10+ guests)	
3	New Distributor Acquisition	
2	New Customer Acquisition	
2	Launch a New Distributor	
	DAILY TOTAL	

DATE:

APPOINTMENTS

am/pm

am/pm

am/pm

am/pm

am/pm

am/pm

am/pm

am/pm

am/pm

am/pm

am/pm

am/pm

am/pm

am/pm

DAILY NOTES

SATURDAY

DAILY METHOD OF OPERATION

Value	Task	Points
1	Pique Someone's Interest	
1	Successful 3 Way Call	
2	Presentation (1 or 2 guests)	
3	Presentation (3+ guests)	
5	Presentation (5+ guests)	
10	Presentation (10+ guests)	
3	New Distributor Acquisition	
2	New Customer Acquisition	
2	Launch a New Distributor	
	DAILY TOTAL	

DATE:

APPOINTMENTS

am/pm   am/pm

am/pm   am/pm

am/pm   am/pm

am/pm   am/pm

am/pm   am/pm

am/pm   am/pm

am/pm   am/pm

DAILY NOTES

SUNDAY

TODAY'S TOP PRIORITIES

DAILY METHOD OF OPERATION

Value	Task	Points
1	Pique Someone's Interest	
1	Successful 3 Way Call	
2	Presentation (1 or 2 guests)	
3	Presentation (3+ guests)	
5	Presentation (5+ guests)	
10	Presentation (10+ guests)	
3	New Distributor Acquisition	
2	New Customer Acquisition	
2	Launch a New Distributor	
	DAILY TOTAL	

DATE:

APPOINTMENTS

_____ am/pm   _____ am/pm

_____ am/pm   _____ am/pm

_____ am/pm   _____ am/pm

_____ am/pm   _____ am/pm

_____ am/pm   _____ am/pm

_____ am/pm   _____ am/pm

_____ am/pm   _____ am/pm

DAILY NOTES

RECAP YOUR PREVIOUS WEEK
AND
PREPARE FOR YOUR NEXT WEEK

REMEMBER: FULL TIME 50+ POINTS   PART TIME 20+ POINTS

DAILY METHOD OF OPERATION TOTALS FOR THE WEEK

Value	Task	Points
1	Pique Someone's Interest	
1	Successful 3 Way Call	
2	Presentation (1 or 2 guests)	
3	Presentation (3+ guests)	
5	Presentation (5+ guests)	
10	Presentation (10+ guests)	
3	New Distributor Acquisition	
2	New Customer Acquisition	
2	Launch a New Distributor	
	WEEKLY TOTAL	

← TOP ACCOMPLISHMENTS FOR THIS PAST WEEK

← THINGS TO IMPROVE ON

GOALS FOR THE COMING WEEK →

IMPORTANT DATES FOR THE COMING WEEK →

MONDAY

DAILY METHOD OF OPERATION

Value	Task	Points
1	Pique Someone's Interest	
1	Successful 3 Way Call	
2	Presentation (1 or 2 guests)	
3	Presentation (3+ guests)	
5	Presentation (5+ guests)	
10	Presentation (10+ guests)	
3	New Distributor Acquisition	
2	New Customer Acquisition	
2	Launch a New Distributor	
	DAILY TOTAL	

DATE:

APPOINTMENTS

am/pm

am/pm

am/pm

am/pm

am/pm

am/pm

am/pm

am/pm

am/pm

am/pm

am/pm

am/pm

am/pm

am/pm

DAILY NOTES

TUESDAY

TODAY'S TOP PRIORITIES

DAILY METHOD OF OPERATION

Value	Task	Points
1	Pique Someone's Interest	
1	Successful 3 Way Call	
2	Presentation (1 or 2 guests)	
3	Presentation (3+ guests)	
5	Presentation (5+ guests)	
10	Presentation (10+ guests)	
3	New Distributor Acquisition	
2	New Customer Acquisition	
2	Launch a New Distributor	
	DAILY TOTAL	

DATE:

APPOINTMENTS

am/pm   am/pm

am/pm   am/pm

am/pm   am/pm

am/pm   am/pm

am/pm   am/pm

am/pm   am/pm

am/pm   am/pm

DAILY NOTES

WEDNESDAY

TODAY'S TOP PRIORITIES

DAILY METHOD OF OPERATION

Value	Task	Points
1	Pique Someone's Interest	
1	Successful 3 Way Call	
2	Presentation (1 or 2 guests)	
3	Presentation (3+ guests)	
5	Presentation (5+ guests)	
10	Presentation (10+ guests)	
3	New Distributor Acquisition	
2	New Customer Acquisition	
2	Launch a New Distributor	
	DAILY TOTAL	

DATE:

APPOINTMENTS

am/pm   am/pm

am/pm   am/pm

am/pm   am/pm

am/pm   am/pm

am/pm   am/pm

am/pm   am/pm

am/pm   am/pm

DAILY NOTES

THURSDAY

TODAY'S TOP PRIORITIES

DAILY METHOD OF OPERATION

Value	Task	Points
1	Pique Someone's Interest	
1	Successful 3 Way Call	
2	Presentation (1 or 2 guests)	
3	Presentation (3+ guests)	
5	Presentation (5+ guests)	
10	Presentation (10+ guests)	
3	New Distributor Acquisition	
2	New Customer Acquisition	
2	Launch a New Distributor	
	DAILY TOTAL	

DATE:

APPOINTMENTS

am/pm _____   am/pm _____

am/pm _____   am/pm _____

am/pm _____   am/pm _____

am/pm _____   am/pm _____

am/pm _____   am/pm _____

am/pm _____   am/pm _____

am/pm _____   am/pm _____

DAILY NOTES

_____

_____

_____

_____

_____

_____

FRIDAY

TODAY'S TOP PRIORITIES

DAILY METHOD OF OPERATION

Value	Task	Points
1	Pique Someone's Interest	
1	Successful 3 Way Call	
2	Presentation (1 or 2 guests)	
3	Presentation (3+ guests)	
5	Presentation (5+ guests)	
10	Presentation (10+ guests)	
3	New Distributor Acquisition	
2	New Customer Acquisition	
2	Launch a New Distributor	
	DAILY TOTAL	

DATE:

APPOINTMENTS

am/pm   am/pm

am/pm   am/pm

am/pm   am/pm

am/pm   am/pm

am/pm   am/pm

am/pm   am/pm

am/pm   am/pm

DAILY NOTES

SATURDAY

DAILY METHOD OF OPERATION

Value	Task	Points
1	Pique Someone's Interest	
1	Successful 3 Way Call	
2	Presentation (1 or 2 guests)	
3	Presentation (3+ guests)	
5	Presentation (5+ guests)	
10	Presentation (10+ guests)	
3	New Distributor Acquisition	
2	New Customer Acquisition	
2	Launch a New Distributor	
	DAILY TOTAL	

DATE:

APPOINTMENTS

am/pm   am/pm

am/pm   am/pm

am/pm   am/pm

am/pm   am/pm

am/pm   am/pm

am/pm   am/pm

am/pm   am/pm

DAILY NOTES

©

SUNDAY

DAILY METHOD OF OPERATION

Value	Task	Points
1	Pique Someone's Interest	
1	Successful 3 Way Call	
2	Presentation (1 or 2 guests)	
3	Presentation (3+ guests)	
5	Presentation (5+ guests)	
10	Presentation (10+ guests)	
3	New Distributor Acquisition	
2	New Customer Acquisition	
2	Launch a New Distributor	
	DAILY TOTAL	

DATE:

APPOINTMENTS

am/pm   am/pm

am/pm   am/pm

am/pm   am/pm

am/pm   am/pm

am/pm   am/pm

am/pm   am/pm

am/pm   am/pm

DAILY NOTES

RECAP YOUR PREVIOUS WEEK
AND
PREPARE FOR YOUR NEXT WEEK

REMEMBER: FULL TIME 50+ POINTS   PART TIME 20+ POINTS

DAILY METHOD OF OPERATION TOTALS FOR THE WEEK

Value	Task	Points
1	Pique Someone's Interest	
1	Successful 3 Way Call	
2	Presentation (1 or 2 guests)	
3	Presentation (3+ guests)	
5	Presentation (5+ guests)	
10	Presentation (10+ guests)	
3	New Distributor Acquisition	
2	New Customer Acquisition	
2	Launch a New Distributor	
	WEEKLY TOTAL	

TOP ACCOMPLISHMENTS FOR THIS PAST WEEK

THINGS TO IMPROVE ON

GOALS FOR THE COMING WEEK

IMPORTANT DATES FOR THE COMING WEEK

MONDAY

TODAY'S TOP PRIORITIES

DAILY METHOD OF OPERATION

Value	Task	Points
1	Pique Someone's Interest	
1	Successful 3 Way Call	
2	Presentation (1 or 2 guests)	
3	Presentation (3+ guests)	
5	Presentation (5+ guests)	
10	Presentation (10+ guests)	
3	New Distributor Acquisition	
2	New Customer Acquisition	
2	Launch a New Distributor	
	DAILY TOTAL	

DATE:

APPOINTMENTS

am/pm _____   am/pm _____

am/pm _____   am/pm _____

am/pm _____   am/pm _____

am/pm _____   am/pm _____

am/pm _____   am/pm _____

am/pm _____   am/pm _____

am/pm _____   am/pm _____

DAILY NOTES

TUESDAY

DAILY METHOD OF OPERATION

Value	Task	Points
1	Pique Someone's Interest	
1	Successful 3 Way Call	
2	Presentation (1 or 2 guests)	
3	Presentation (3+ guests)	
5	Presentation (5+ guests)	
10	Presentation (10+ guests)	
3	New Distributor Acquisition	
2	New Customer Acquisition	
2	Launch a New Distributor	
	DAILY TOTAL	

DATE:

APPOINTMENTS

am/pm   am/pm

am/pm   am/pm

am/pm   am/pm

am/pm   am/pm

am/pm   am/pm

am/pm   am/pm

am/pm   am/pm

DAILY NOTES

WEDNESDAY

TODAY'S TOP PRIORITIES

DAILY METHOD OF OPERATION

Value	Task	Points
1	Pique Someone's Interest	
1	Successful 3 Way Call	
2	Presentation (1 or 2 guests)	
3	Presentation (3+ guests)	
5	Presentation (5+ guests)	
10	Presentation (10+ guests)	
3	New Distributor Acquisition	
2	New Customer Acquisition	
2	Launch a New Distributor	
	DAILY TOTAL	

DATE:

APPOINTMENTS

_____ am/pm _____   _____ am/pm _____

_____ am/pm _____   _____ am/pm _____

_____ am/pm _____   _____ am/pm _____

_____ am/pm _____   _____ am/pm _____

_____ am/pm _____   _____ am/pm _____

_____ am/pm _____   _____ am/pm _____

_____ am/pm _____   _____ am/pm _____

DAILY NOTES

THURSDAY

TODAY'S TOP PRIORITIES

DAILY METHOD OF OPERATION

Value	Task	Points
1	Pique Someone's Interest	
1	Successful 3 Way Call	
2	Presentation (1 or 2 guests)	
3	Presentation (3+ guests)	
5	Presentation (5+ guests)	
10	Presentation (10+ guests)	
3	New Distributor Acquisition	
2	New Customer Acquisition	
2	Launch a New Distributor	
	DAILY TOTAL	

DATE:

APPOINTMENTS

am/pm   am/pm

am/pm   am/pm

am/pm   am/pm

am/pm   am/pm

am/pm   am/pm

am/pm   am/pm

am/pm   am/pm

DAILY NOTES

FRIDAY

TODAY'S TOP PRIORITIES

DAILY METHOD OF OPERATION

Value	Task	Points
1	Pique Someone's Interest	
1	Successful 3 Way Call	
2	Presentation (1 or 2 guests)	
3	Presentation (3+ guests)	
5	Presentation (5+ guests)	
10	Presentation (10+ guests)	
3	New Distributor Acquisition	
2	New Customer Acquisition	
2	Launch a New Distributor	
	DAILY TOTAL	

DATE:

APPOINTMENTS

am/pm   am/pm

am/pm   am/pm

am/pm   am/pm

am/pm   am/pm

am/pm   am/pm

am/pm   am/pm

am/pm   am/pm

DAILY NOTES

SATURDAY

DAILY METHOD OF OPERATION

Value	Task	Points
1	Pique Someone's Interest	
1	Successful 3 Way Call	
2	Presentation (1 or 2 guests)	
3	Presentation (3+ guests)	
5	Presentation (5+ guests)	
10	Presentation (10+ guests)	
3	New Distributor Acquisition	
2	New Customer Acquisition	
2	Launch a New Distributor	
	DAILY TOTAL	

DATE:

APPOINTMENTS

am/pm   am/pm

am/pm   am/pm

am/pm   am/pm

am/pm   am/pm

am/pm   am/pm

am/pm   am/pm

am/pm   am/pm

DAILY NOTES

SUNDAY

DAILY METHOD OF OPERATION

Value	Task	Points
1	Pique Someone's Interest	
1	Successful 3 Way Call	
2	Presentation (1 or 2 guests)	
3	Presentation (3+ guests)	
5	Presentation (5+ guests)	
10	Presentation (10+ guests)	
3	New Distributor Acquisition	
2	New Customer Acquisition	
2	Launch a New Distributor	
	DAILY TOTAL	

DATE:

APPOINTMENTS

_____ am/pm _____   _____ am/pm _____

_____ am/pm _____   _____ am/pm _____

_____ am/pm _____   _____ am/pm _____

_____ am/pm _____   _____ am/pm _____

_____ am/pm _____   _____ am/pm _____

_____ am/pm _____   _____ am/pm _____

_____ am/pm _____   _____ am/pm _____

DAILY NOTES

_____

_____

_____

_____

_____

_____

RECAP YOUR PREVIOUS WEEK

AND

PREPARE FOR YOUR NEXT WEEK

REMEMBER: FULL TIME 50+ POINTS   PART TIME 20+ POINTS

DAILY METHOD OF OPERATION TOTALS FOR THE WEEK

Value	Task	Points
1	Pique Someone's Interest	
1	Successful 3 Way Call	
2	Presentation (1 or 2 guests)	
3	Presentation (3+ guests)	
5	Presentation (5+ guests)	
10	Presentation (10+ guests)	
3	New Distributor Acquisition	
2	New Customer Acquisition	
2	Launch a New Distributor	
	WEEKLY TOTAL	

← TOP ACCOMPLISHMENTS FOR THIS PAST WEEK

← THINGS TO IMPROVE ON

GOALS FOR THE COMING WEEK →

IMPORTANT DATES FOR THE COMING WEEK →

MONDAY

TODAY'S TOP PRIORITIES

DAILY METHOD OF OPERATION

Value	Task	Points
1	Pique Someone's Interest	
1	Successful 3 Way Call	
2	Presentation (1 or 2 guests)	
3	Presentation (3+ guests)	
5	Presentation (5+ guests)	
10	Presentation (10+ guests)	
3	New Distributor Acquisition	
2	New Customer Acquisition	
2	Launch a New Distributor	
	DAILY TOTAL	

DATE:

APPOINTMENTS

_____ am/pm _____   _____ am/pm _____

_____ am/pm _____   _____ am/pm _____

_____ am/pm _____   _____ am/pm _____

_____ am/pm _____   _____ am/pm _____

_____ am/pm _____   _____ am/pm _____

_____ am/pm _____   _____ am/pm _____

_____ am/pm _____   _____ am/pm _____

DAILY NOTES

TUESDAY

TODAY'S TOP PRIORITIES

DAILY METHOD OF OPERATION

Value	Task	Points
1	Pique Someone's Interest	
1	Successful 3 Way Call	
2	Presentation (1 or 2 guests)	
3	Presentation (3+ guests)	
5	Presentation (5+ guests)	
10	Presentation (10+ guests)	
3	New Distributor Acquisition	
2	New Customer Acquisition	
2	Launch a New Distributor	
	DAILY TOTAL	

DATE:

APPOINTMENTS

am/pm _____   am/pm _____

am/pm _____   am/pm _____

am/pm _____   am/pm _____

am/pm _____   am/pm _____

am/pm _____   am/pm _____

am/pm _____   am/pm _____

am/pm _____   am/pm _____

DAILY NOTES

_____

_____

_____

_____

_____

_____

WEDNESDAY

DAILY METHOD OF OPERATION

Value	Task	Points
1	Pique Someone's Interest	
1	Successful 3 Way Call	
2	Presentation (1 or 2 guests)	
3	Presentation (3+ guests)	
5	Presentation (5+ guests)	
10	Presentation (10+ guests)	
3	New Distributor Acquisition	
2	New Customer Acquisition	
2	Launch a New Distributor	
	DAILY TOTAL	

DATE:

APPOINTMENTS

am/pm   am/pm

am/pm   am/pm

am/pm   am/pm

am/pm   am/pm

am/pm   am/pm

am/pm   am/pm

am/pm   am/pm

DAILY NOTES

THURSDAY

TODAY'S TOP PRIORITIES

DAILY METHOD OF OPERATION

Value	Task	Points
1	Pique Someone's Interest	
1	Successful 3 Way Call	
2	Presentation (1 or 2 guests)	
3	Presentation (3+ guests)	
5	Presentation (5+ guests)	
10	Presentation (10+ guests)	
3	New Distributor Acquisition	
2	New Customer Acquisition	
2	Launch a New Distributor	
	DAILY TOTAL	

DATE:

APPOINTMENTS

am/pm   am/pm

am/pm   am/pm

am/pm   am/pm

am/pm   am/pm

am/pm   am/pm

am/pm   am/pm

am/pm   am/pm

DAILY NOTES

FRIDAY

TODAY'S TOP PRIORITIES

DAILY METHOD OF OPERATION

Value	Task	Points
1	Pique Someone's Interest	
1	Successful 3 Way Call	
2	Presentation (1 or 2 guests)	
3	Presentation (3+ guests)	
5	Presentation (5+ guests)	
10	Presentation (10+ guests)	
3	New Distributor Acquisition	
2	New Customer Acquisition	
2	Launch a New Distributor	
	DAILY TOTAL	

DATE:

APPOINTMENTS

am/pm   am/pm

am/pm   am/pm

am/pm   am/pm

am/pm   am/pm

am/pm   am/pm

am/pm   am/pm

am/pm   am/pm

DAILY NOTES

SATURDAY

TODAY'S TOP PRIORITIES

DAILY METHOD OF OPERATION

Value	Task	Points
1	Pique Someone's Interest	
1	Successful 3 Way Call	
2	Presentation (1 or 2 guests)	
3	Presentation (3+ guests)	
5	Presentation (5+ guests)	
10	Presentation (10+ guests)	
3	New Distributor Acquisition	
2	New Customer Acquisition	
2	Launch a New Distributor	
	DAILY TOTAL	

DATE:

APPOINTMENTS

am/pm   am/pm

am/pm   am/pm

am/pm   am/pm

am/pm   am/pm

am/pm   am/pm

am/pm   am/pm

am/pm   am/pm

DAILY NOTES

SUNDAY

TODAY'S TOP PRIORITIES

DAILY METHOD OF OPERATION

Value	Task	Points
1	Pique Someone's Interest	
1	Successful 3 Way Call	
2	Presentation (1 or 2 guests)	
3	Presentation (3+ guests)	
5	Presentation (5+ guests)	
10	Presentation (10+ guests)	
3	New Distributor Acquisition	
2	New Customer Acquisition	
2	Launch a New Distributor	
	DAILY TOTAL	

DATE:

APPOINTMENTS

am/pm   am/pm

am/pm   am/pm

am/pm   am/pm

am/pm   am/pm

am/pm   am/pm

am/pm   am/pm

am/pm   am/pm

DAILY NOTES

RECAP YOUR PREVIOUS WEEK
AND
PREPARE FOR YOUR NEXT WEEK

REMEMBER: FULL TIME 50+ POINTS   PART TIME 20+ POINTS

DAILY METHOD OF OPERATION TOTALS FOR THE WEEK

Value	Task	Points
1	Pique Someone's Interest	
1	Successful 3 Way Call	
2	Presentation (1 or 2 guests)	
3	Presentation (3+ guests)	
5	Presentation (5+ guests)	
10	Presentation (10+ guests)	
3	New Distributor Acquisition	
2	New Customer Acquisition	
2	Launch a New Distributor	
	WEEKLY TOTAL	

TOP ACCOMPLISHMENTS FOR THIS PAST WEEK

THINGS TO IMPROVE ON

GOALS FOR THE COMING WEEK

IMPORTANT DATES FOR THE COMING WEEK

MONDAY

TODAY'S TOP PRIORITIES

DAILY METHOD OF OPERATION

Value	Task	Points
1	Pique Someone's Interest	
1	Successful 3 Way Call	
2	Presentation (1 or 2 guests)	
3	Presentation (3+ guests)	
5	Presentation (5+ guests)	
10	Presentation (10+ guests)	
3	New Distributor Acquisition	
2	New Customer Acquisition	
2	Launch a New Distributor	
	DAILY TOTAL	

DATE:

APPOINTMENTS

am/pm

am/pm

am/pm

am/pm

am/pm

am/pm

am/pm

am/pm

am/pm

am/pm

am/pm

am/pm

am/pm

am/pm

DAILY NOTES

TUESDAY

DAILY METHOD OF OPERATION

Value	Task	Points
1	Pique Someone's Interest	
1	Successful 3 Way Call	
2	Presentation (1 or 2 guests)	
3	Presentation (3+ guests)	
5	Presentation (5+ guests)	
10	Presentation (10+ guests)	
3	New Distributor Acquisition	
2	New Customer Acquisition	
2	Launch a New Distributor	
	DAILY TOTAL	

DATE:

APPOINTMENTS

am/pm   am/pm

am/pm   am/pm

am/pm   am/pm

am/pm   am/pm

am/pm   am/pm

am/pm   am/pm

am/pm   am/pm

DAILY NOTES

WEDNESDAY

DAILY METHOD OF OPERATION

Value	Task	Points
1	Pique Someone's Interest	
1	Successful 3 Way Call	
2	Presentation (1 or 2 guests)	
3	Presentation (3+ guests)	
5	Presentation (5+ guests)	
10	Presentation (10+ guests)	
3	New Distributor Acquisition	
2	New Customer Acquisition	
2	Launch a New Distributor	
	DAILY TOTAL	

DATE:

APPOINTMENTS

am/pm   am/pm

am/pm   am/pm

am/pm   am/pm

am/pm   am/pm

am/pm   am/pm

am/pm   am/pm

am/pm   am/pm

DAILY NOTES

THURSDAY

TODAY'S TOP PRIORITIES

DAILY METHOD OF OPERATION

Value	Task	Points
1	Pique Someone's Interest	
1	Successful 3 Way Call	
2	Presentation (1 or 2 guests)	
3	Presentation (3+ guests)	
5	Presentation (5+ guests)	
10	Presentation (10+ guests)	
3	New Distributor Acquisition	
2	New Customer Acquisition	
2	Launch a New Distributor	
	DAILY TOTAL	

DATE:

APPOINTMENTS

am/pm	am/pm
am/pm	am/pm
am/pm	am/pm
am/pm	am/pm
am/pm	am/pm
am/pm	am/pm
am/pm	am/pm

DAILY NOTES

FRIDAY

TODAY'S TOP PRIORITIES

DAILY METHOD OF OPERATION

Value	Task	Points
1	Pique Someone's Interest	
1	Successful 3 Way Call	
2	Presentation (1 or 2 guests)	
3	Presentation (3+ guests)	
5	Presentation (5+ guests)	
10	Presentation (10+ guests)	
3	New Distributor Acquisition	
2	New Customer Acquisition	
2	Launch a New Distributor	
	DAILY TOTAL	

DATE:

APPOINTMENTS

am/pm   am/pm

am/pm   am/pm

am/pm   am/pm

am/pm   am/pm

am/pm   am/pm

am/pm   am/pm

am/pm   am/pm

DAILY NOTES

SATURDAY

DAILY METHOD OF OPERATION

Value	Task	Points
1	Pique Someone's Interest	
1	Successful 3 Way Call	
2	Presentation (1 or 2 guests)	
3	Presentation (3+ guests)	
5	Presentation (5+ guests)	
10	Presentation (10+ guests)	
3	New Distributor Acquisition	
2	New Customer Acquisition	
2	Launch a New Distributor	
	DAILY TOTAL	

DATE:

APPOINTMENTS

am/pm   am/pm

am/pm   am/pm

am/pm   am/pm

am/pm   am/pm

am/pm   am/pm

am/pm   am/pm

am/pm   am/pm

DAILY NOTES

SUNDAY

TODAY'S TOP PRIORITIES

DAILY METHOD OF OPERATION

Value	Task	Points
1	Pique Someone's Interest	
1	Successful 3 Way Call	
2	Presentation (1 or 2 guests)	
3	Presentation (3+ guests)	
5	Presentation (5+ guests)	
10	Presentation (10+ guests)	
3	New Distributor Acquisition	
2	New Customer Acquisition	
2	Launch a New Distributor	
	DAILY TOTAL	

DATE:

APPOINTMENTS

am/pm   am/pm

am/pm   am/pm

am/pm   am/pm

am/pm   am/pm

am/pm   am/pm

am/pm   am/pm

am/pm   am/pm

DAILY NOTES

RECAP YOUR PREVIOUS WEEK
AND
PREPARE FOR YOUR NEXT WEEK

REMEMBER: FULL TIME 50+ POINTS   PART TIME 20+ POINTS

DAILY METHOD OF OPERATION TOTALS FOR THE WEEK

Value	Task	Points
1	Pique Someone's Interest	
1	Successful 3 Way Call	
2	Presentation (1 or 2 guests)	
3	Presentation (3+ guests)	
5	Presentation (5+ guests)	
10	Presentation (10+ guests)	
3	New Distributor Acquisition	
2	New Customer Acquisition	
2	Launch a New Distributor	
	WEEKLY TOTAL	

← TOP ACCOMPLISHMENTS FOR THIS PAST WEEK

← THINGS TO IMPROVE ON

GOALS FOR THE COMING WEEK →

IMPORTANT DATES FOR THE COMING WEEK →

MONDAY

TODAY'S TOP PRIORITIES

DAILY METHOD OF OPERATION

Value	Task	Points
1	Pique Someone's Interest	
1	Successful 3 Way Call	
2	Presentation (1 or 2 guests)	
3	Presentation (3+ guests)	
5	Presentation (5+ guests)	
10	Presentation (10+ guests)	
3	New Distributor Acquisition	
2	New Customer Acquisition	
2	Launch a New Distributor	
	DAILY TOTAL	

DATE:

APPOINTMENTS

_____ am/pm _____   _____ am/pm _____

_____ am/pm _____   _____ am/pm _____

_____ am/pm _____   _____ am/pm _____

_____ am/pm _____   _____ am/pm _____

_____ am/pm _____   _____ am/pm _____

_____ am/pm _____   _____ am/pm _____

_____ am/pm _____   _____ am/pm _____

DAILY NOTES

TUESDAY

DAILY METHOD OF OPERATION

Value	Task	Points
1	Pique Someone's Interest	
1	Successful 3 Way Call	
2	Presentation (1 or 2 guests)	
3	Presentation (3+ guests)	
5	Presentation (5+ guests)	
10	Presentation (10+ guests)	
3	New Distributor Acquisition	
2	New Customer Acquisition	
2	Launch a New Distributor	
	DAILY TOTAL	

DATE:

APPOINTMENTS

am/pm   am/pm

am/pm   am/pm

am/pm   am/pm

am/pm   am/pm

am/pm   am/pm

am/pm   am/pm

am/pm   am/pm

DAILY NOTES

WEDNESDAY

TODAY'S TOP PRIORITIES

DAILY METHOD OF OPERATION

Value	Task	Points
1	Pique Someone's Interest	
1	Successful 3 Way Call	
2	Presentation (1 or 2 guests)	
3	Presentation (3+ guests)	
5	Presentation (5+ guests)	
10	Presentation (10+ guests)	
3	New Distributor Acquisition	
2	New Customer Acquisition	
2	Launch a New Distributor	
	DAILY TOTAL	

DATE:

APPOINTMENTS

am/pm   am/pm

am/pm   am/pm

am/pm   am/pm

am/pm   am/pm

am/pm   am/pm

am/pm   am/pm

am/pm   am/pm

DAILY NOTES

THURSDAY

DAILY METHOD OF OPERATION

Value	Task	Points
1	Pique Someone's Interest	
1	Successful 3 Way Call	
2	Presentation (1 or 2 guests)	
3	Presentation (3+ guests)	
5	Presentation (5+ guests)	
10	Presentation (10+ guests)	
3	New Distributor Acquisition	
2	New Customer Acquisition	
2	Launch a New Distributor	
	DAILY TOTAL	

DATE:

APPOINTMENTS

am/pm   am/pm

am/pm   am/pm

am/pm   am/pm

am/pm   am/pm

am/pm   am/pm

am/pm   am/pm

am/pm   am/pm

DAILY NOTES

FRIDAY

TODAY'S TOP PRIORITIES

DAILY METHOD OF OPERATION

Value	Task	Points
1	Pique Someone's Interest	
1	Successful 3 Way Call	
2	Presentation (1 or 2 guests)	
3	Presentation (3+ guests)	
5	Presentation (5+ guests)	
10	Presentation (10+ guests)	
3	New Distributor Acquisition	
2	New Customer Acquisition	
2	Launch a New Distributor	
	DAILY TOTAL	

DATE:

APPOINTMENTS

am/pm   am/pm

am/pm   am/pm

am/pm   am/pm

am/pm   am/pm

am/pm   am/pm

am/pm   am/pm

am/pm   am/pm

DAILY NOTES

SATURDAY

DAILY METHOD OF OPERATION

Value	Task	Points
1	Pique Someone's Interest	
1	Successful 3 Way Call	
2	Presentation (1 or 2 guests)	
3	Presentation (3+ guests)	
5	Presentation (5+ guests)	
10	Presentation (10+ guests)	
3	New Distributor Acquisition	
2	New Customer Acquisition	
2	Launch a New Distributor	
	DAILY TOTAL	

DATE:

APPOINTMENTS

am/pm   am/pm

am/pm   am/pm

am/pm   am/pm

am/pm   am/pm

am/pm   am/pm

am/pm   am/pm

am/pm   am/pm

DAILY NOTES

SUNDAY

TODAY'S TOP PRIORITIES

DAILY METHOD OF OPERATION

Value	Task	Points
1	Pique Someone's Interest	
1	Successful 3 Way Call	
2	Presentation (1 or 2 guests)	
3	Presentation (3+ guests)	
5	Presentation (5+ guests)	
10	Presentation (10+ guests)	
3	New Distributor Acquisition	
2	New Customer Acquisition	
2	Launch a New Distributor	
	DAILY TOTAL	

DATE:

APPOINTMENTS

am/pm
am/pm

am/pm
am/pm

am/pm
am/pm

am/pm
am/pm

am/pm
am/pm

am/pm
am/pm

am/pm
am/pm

DAILY NOTES

RECAP YOUR PREVIOUS WEEK
AND
PREPARE FOR YOUR NEXT WEEK

REMEMBER: FULL TIME 50+ POINTS PART TIME 20+ POINTS

DAILY METHOD OF OPERATION TOTALS FOR THE WEEK

Value	Task	Points
1	Pique Someone's Interest	
1	Successful 3 Way Call	
2	Presentation (1 or 2 guests)	
3	Presentation (3+ guests)	
5	Presentation (5+ guests)	
10	Presentation (10+ guests)	
3	New Distributor Acquisition	
2	New Customer Acquisition	
2	Launch a New Distributor	
	WEEKLY TOTAL	

TOP ACCOMPLISHMENTS FOR THIS PAST WEEK

←

THINGS TO IMPROVE ON

←

GOALS FOR THE COMING WEEK

→

IMPORTANT DATES FOR THE COMING WEEK

→

MONDAY

TODAY'S TOP PRIORITIES

DAILY METHOD OF OPERATION

Value	Task	Points
1	Pique Someone's Interest	
1	Successful 3 Way Call	
2	Presentation (1 or 2 guests)	
3	Presentation (3+ guests)	
5	Presentation (5+ guests)	
10	Presentation (10+ guests)	
3	New Distributor Acquisition	
2	New Customer Acquisition	
2	Launch a New Distributor	
	DAILY TOTAL	

DATE:

APPOINTMENTS

am/pm	am/pm
am/pm	am/pm
am/pm	am/pm
am/pm	am/pm
am/pm	am/pm
am/pm	am/pm
am/pm	am/pm

DAILY NOTES

TUESDAY

TODAY'S TOP PRIORITIES

DAILY METHOD OF OPERATION

Value	Task	Points
1	Pique Someone's Interest	
1	Successful 3 Way Call	
2	Presentation (1 or 2 guests)	
3	Presentation (3+ guests)	
5	Presentation (5+ guests)	
10	Presentation (10+ guests)	
3	New Distributor Acquisition	
2	New Customer Acquisition	
2	Launch a New Distributor	
	DAILY TOTAL	

DATE:

APPOINTMENTS

am/pm   am/pm

am/pm   am/pm

am/pm   am/pm

am/pm   am/pm

am/pm   am/pm

am/pm   am/pm

am/pm   am/pm

DAILY NOTES

WEDNESDAY

TODAY'S TOP PRIORITIES

DAILY METHOD OF OPERATION

Value	Task	Points
1	Pique Someone's Interest	
1	Successful 3 Way Call	
2	Presentation (1 or 2 guests)	
3	Presentation (3+ guests)	
5	Presentation (5+ guests)	
10	Presentation (10+ guests)	
3	New Distributor Acquisition	
2	New Customer Acquisition	
2	Launch a New Distributor	
	DAILY TOTAL	

DATE:

APPOINTMENTS

am/pm

am/pm

am/pm

am/pm

am/pm

am/pm

am/pm

am/pm

am/pm

am/pm

am/pm

am/pm

am/pm

am/pm

DAILY NOTES

THURSDAY

TODAY'S TOP PRIORITIES

DAILY METHOD OF OPERATION

Value	Task	Points
1	Pique Someone's Interest	
1	Successful 3 Way Call	
2	Presentation (1 or 2 guests)	
3	Presentation (3+ guests)	
5	Presentation (5+ guests)	
10	Presentation (10+ guests)	
3	New Distributor Acquisition	
2	New Customer Acquisition	
2	Launch a New Distributor	
	DAILY TOTAL	

DATE:

APPOINTMENTS

am/pm   am/pm

am/pm   am/pm

am/pm   am/pm

am/pm   am/pm

am/pm   am/pm

am/pm   am/pm

am/pm   am/pm

DAILY NOTES

FRIDAY

DAILY METHOD OF OPERATION

Value	Task	Points
1	Pique Someone's Interest	
1	Successful 3 Way Call	
2	Presentation (1 or 2 guests)	
3	Presentation (3+ guests)	
5	Presentation (5+ guests)	
10	Presentation (10+ guests)	
3	New Distributor Acquisition	
2	New Customer Acquisition	
2	Launch a New Distributor	
	DAILY TOTAL	

DATE:

APPOINTMENTS

am/pm   am/pm

am/pm   am/pm

am/pm   am/pm

am/pm   am/pm

am/pm   am/pm

am/pm   am/pm

am/pm   am/pm

DAILY NOTES

SATURDAY

TODAY'S TOP PRIORITIES

DAILY METHOD OF OPERATION

Value	Task	Points
1	Pique Someone's Interest	
1	Successful 3 Way Call	
2	Presentation (1 or 2 guests)	
3	Presentation (3+ guests)	
5	Presentation (5+ guests)	
10	Presentation (10+ guests)	
3	New Distributor Acquisition	
2	New Customer Acquisition	
2	Launch a New Distributor	
	DAILY TOTAL	

DATE:

APPOINTMENTS

am/pm   am/pm

am/pm   am/pm

am/pm   am/pm

am/pm   am/pm

am/pm   am/pm

am/pm   am/pm

am/pm   am/pm

DAILY NOTES

SUNDAY

TODAY'S TOP PRIORITIES

DAILY METHOD OF OPERATION

Value	Task	Points
1	Pique Someone's Interest	
1	Successful 3 Way Call	
2	Presentation (1 or 2 guests)	
3	Presentation (3+ guests)	
5	Presentation (5+ guests)	
10	Presentation (10+ guests)	
3	New Distributor Acquisition	
2	New Customer Acquisition	
2	Launch a New Distributor	
	DAILY TOTAL	

DATE:

APPOINTMENTS

am/pm   am/pm

am/pm   am/pm

am/pm   am/pm

am/pm   am/pm

am/pm   am/pm

am/pm   am/pm

am/pm   am/pm

DAILY NOTES

RECAP YOUR PREVIOUS WEEK
AND
PREPARE FOR YOUR NEXT WEEK

REMEMBER: FULL TIME 50+ POINTS   PART TIME 20+ POINTS

DAILY METHOD OF OPERATION TOTALS FOR THE WEEK

Value	Task	Points
1	Pique Someone's Interest	
1	Successful 3 Way Call	
2	Presentation (1 or 2 guests)	
3	Presentation (3+ guests)	
5	Presentation (5+ guests)	
10	Presentation (10+ guests)	
3	New Distributor Acquisition	
2	New Customer Acquisition	
2	Launch a New Distributor	
	WEEKLY TOTAL	

← **TOP ACCOMPLISHMENTS FOR THIS PAST WEEK**

← **THINGS TO IMPROVE ON**

GOALS FOR THE COMING WEEK →

IMPORTANT DATES FOR THE COMING WEEK →

MONDAY

TODAY'S TOP PRIORITIES

DAILY METHOD OF OPERATION

Value	Task	Points
1	Pique Someone's Interest	
1	Successful 3 Way Call	
2	Presentation (1 or 2 guests)	
3	Presentation (3+ guests)	
5	Presentation (5+ guests)	
10	Presentation (10+ guests)	
3	New Distributor Acquisition	
2	New Customer Acquisition	
2	Launch a New Distributor	
	DAILY TOTAL	

DATE:

APPOINTMENTS

am/pm   am/pm

am/pm   am/pm

am/pm   am/pm

am/pm   am/pm

am/pm   am/pm

am/pm   am/pm

am/pm   am/pm

DAILY NOTES

TUESDAY

DAILY METHOD OF OPERATION

Value	Task	Points
1	Pique Someone's Interest	
1	Successful 3 Way Call	
2	Presentation (1 or 2 guests)	
3	Presentation (3+ guests)	
5	Presentation (5+ guests)	
10	Presentation (10+ guests)	
3	New Distributor Acquisition	
2	New Customer Acquisition	
2	Launch a New Distributor	
	DAILY TOTAL	

DATE:

APPOINTMENTS

am/pm   am/pm

am/pm   am/pm

am/pm   am/pm

am/pm   am/pm

am/pm   am/pm

am/pm   am/pm

am/pm   am/pm

DAILY NOTES

WEDNESDAY

DAILY METHOD OF OPERATION

Value	Task	Points
1	Pique Someone's Interest	
1	Successful 3 Way Call	
2	Presentation (1 or 2 guests)	
3	Presentation (3+ guests)	
5	Presentation (5+ guests)	
10	Presentation (10+ guests)	
3	New Distributor Acquisition	
2	New Customer Acquisition	
2	Launch a New Distributor	
	DAILY TOTAL	

DATE:

APPOINTMENTS

am/pm   am/pm

am/pm   am/pm

am/pm   am/pm

am/pm   am/pm

am/pm   am/pm

am/pm   am/pm

am/pm   am/pm

DAILY NOTES

THURSDAY

TODAY'S TOP PRIORITIES

DAILY METHOD OF OPERATION

Value	Task	Points
1	Pique Someone's Interest	
1	Successful 3 Way Call	
2	Presentation (1 or 2 guests)	
3	Presentation (3+ guests)	
5	Presentation (5+ guests)	
10	Presentation (10+ guests)	
3	New Distributor Acquisition	
2	New Customer Acquisition	
2	Launch a New Distributor	
	DAILY TOTAL	

DATE:

APPOINTMENTS

---

am/pm _____   am/pm _____

am/pm _____   am/pm _____

am/pm _____   am/pm _____

am/pm _____   am/pm _____

am/pm _____   am/pm _____

am/pm _____   am/pm _____

am/pm _____   am/pm _____

DAILY NOTES

_____

_____

_____

_____

_____

_____

FRIDAY

DAILY METHOD OF OPERATION

Value	Task	Points
1	Pique Someone's Interest	
1	Successful 3 Way Call	
2	Presentation (1 or 2 guests)	
3	Presentation (3+ guests)	
5	Presentation (5+ guests)	
10	Presentation (10+ guests)	
3	New Distributor Acquisition	
2	New Customer Acquisition	
2	Launch a New Distributor	
	DAILY TOTAL	

DATE:

APPOINTMENTS

am/pm

am/pm

am/pm

am/pm

am/pm

am/pm

am/pm

am/pm

am/pm

am/pm

am/pm

am/pm

am/pm

am/pm

DAILY NOTES

SATURDAY

TODAY'S TOP PRIORITIES

DAILY METHOD OF OPERATION

Value	Task	Points
1	Pique Someone's Interest	
1	Successful 3 Way Call	
2	Presentation (1 or 2 guests)	
3	Presentation (3+ guests)	
5	Presentation (5+ guests)	
10	Presentation (10+ guests)	
3	New Distributor Acquisition	
2	New Customer Acquisition	
2	Launch a New Distributor	
	DAILY TOTAL	

DATE:

APPOINTMENTS

am/pm	am/pm
am/pm	am/pm
am/pm	am/pm
am/pm	am/pm
am/pm	am/pm
am/pm	am/pm
am/pm	am/pm

DAILY NOTES

SUNDAY

TODAY'S TOP PRIORITIES

DAILY METHOD OF OPERATION

Value	Task	Points
1	Pique Someone's Interest	
1	Successful 3 Way Call	
2	Presentation (1 or 2 guests)	
3	Presentation (3+ guests)	
5	Presentation (5+ guests)	
10	Presentation (10+ guests)	
3	New Distributor Acquisition	
2	New Customer Acquisition	
2	Launch a New Distributor	
	DAILY TOTAL	

DATE:

APPOINTMENTS

am/pm   am/pm

am/pm   am/pm

am/pm   am/pm

am/pm   am/pm

am/pm   am/pm

am/pm   am/pm

am/pm   am/pm

DAILY NOTES

RECAP YOUR PREVIOUS WEEK
AND
PREPARE FOR YOUR NEXT WEEK

REMEMBER: FULL TIME 50+ POINTS   PART TIME 20+ POINTS

DAILY METHOD OF OPERATION TOTALS FOR THE WEEK

Value	Task	Points
1	Pique Someone's Interest	
1	Successful 3 Way Call	
2	Presentation (1 or 2 guests)	
3	Presentation (3+ guests)	
5	Presentation (5+ guests)	
10	Presentation (10+ guests)	
3	New Distributor Acquisition	
2	New Customer Acquisition	
2	Launch a New Distributor	
	WEEKLY TOTAL	

← **TOP ACCOMPLISHMENTS FOR THIS PAST WEEK**

← **THINGS TO IMPROVE ON**

GOALS FOR THE COMING WEEK →

IMPORTANT DATES FOR THE COMING WEEK →

MONDAY

TODAY'S TOP PRIORITIES

DAILY METHOD OF OPERATION

Value	Task	Points
1	Pique Someone's Interest	
1	Successful 3 Way Call	
2	Presentation (1 or 2 guests)	
3	Presentation (3+ guests)	
5	Presentation (5+ guests)	
10	Presentation (10+ guests)	
3	New Distributor Acquisition	
2	New Customer Acquisition	
2	Launch a New Distributor	
	DAILY TOTAL	

DATE:

APPOINTMENTS

am/pm   am/pm

am/pm   am/pm

am/pm   am/pm

am/pm   am/pm

am/pm   am/pm

am/pm   am/pm

am/pm   am/pm

DAILY NOTES

TUESDAY

DAILY METHOD OF OPERATION

Value	Task	Points
1	Pique Someone's Interest	
1	Successful 3 Way Call	
2	Presentation (1 or 2 guests)	
3	Presentation (3+ guests)	
5	Presentation (5+ guests)	
10	Presentation (10+ guests)	
3	New Distributor Acquisition	
2	New Customer Acquisition	
2	Launch a New Distributor	
	DAILY TOTAL	

DATE:

APPOINTMENTS

am/pm   am/pm

am/pm   am/pm

am/pm   am/pm

am/pm   am/pm

am/pm   am/pm

am/pm   am/pm

am/pm   am/pm

DAILY NOTES

WEDNESDAY

DAILY METHOD OF OPERATION

Value	Task	Points
1	Pique Someone's Interest	
1	Successful 3 Way Call	
2	Presentation (1 or 2 guests)	
3	Presentation (3+ guests)	
5	Presentation (5+ guests)	
10	Presentation (10+ guests)	
3	New Distributor Acquisition	
2	New Customer Acquisition	
2	Launch a New Distributor	
	DAILY TOTAL	

DATE:

APPOINTMENTS

am/pm

am/pm

am/pm

am/pm

am/pm

am/pm

am/pm

am/pm

am/pm

am/pm

am/pm

am/pm

am/pm

am/pm

DAILY NOTES

THURSDAY

DAILY METHOD OF OPERATION

Value	Task	Points
1	Pique Someone's Interest	
1	Successful 3 Way Call	
2	Presentation (1 or 2 guests)	
3	Presentation (3+ guests)	
5	Presentation (5+ guests)	
10	Presentation (10+ guests)	
3	New Distributor Acquisition	
2	New Customer Acquisition	
2	Launch a New Distributor	
	DAILY TOTAL	

DATE:

APPOINTMENTS

am/pm _____   am/pm _____

am/pm _____   am/pm _____

am/pm _____   am/pm _____

am/pm _____   am/pm _____

am/pm _____   am/pm _____

am/pm _____   am/pm _____

am/pm _____   am/pm _____

DAILY NOTES

_____

_____

_____

_____

_____

_____

FRIDAY

DAILY METHOD OF OPERATION

Value	Task	Points
1	Pique Someone's Interest	
1	Successful 3 Way Call	
2	Presentation (1 or 2 guests)	
3	Presentation (3+ guests)	
5	Presentation (5+ guests)	
10	Presentation (10+ guests)	
3	New Distributor Acquisition	
2	New Customer Acquisition	
2	Launch a New Distributor	
	DAILY TOTAL	

DATE:

APPOINTMENTS

am/pm

am/pm

am/pm

am/pm

am/pm

am/pm

am/pm

am/pm

am/pm

am/pm

am/pm

am/pm

am/pm

am/pm

DAILY NOTES

SATURDAY

DAILY METHOD OF OPERATION

Value	Task	Points
1	Pique Someone's Interest	
1	Successful 3 Way Call	
2	Presentation (1 or 2 guests)	
3	Presentation (3+ guests)	
5	Presentation (5+ guests)	
10	Presentation (10+ guests)	
3	New Distributor Acquisition	
2	New Customer Acquisition	
2	Launch a New Distributor	
	DAILY TOTAL	

DATE:

APPOINTMENTS

am/pm   am/pm

am/pm   am/pm

am/pm   am/pm

am/pm   am/pm

am/pm   am/pm

am/pm   am/pm

am/pm   am/pm

DAILY NOTES

SUNDAY

TODAY'S TOP PRIORITIES

DAILY METHOD OF OPERATION

Value	Task	Points
1	Pique Someone's Interest	
1	Successful 3 Way Call	
2	Presentation (1 or 2 guests)	
3	Presentation (3+ guests)	
5	Presentation (5+ guests)	
10	Presentation (10+ guests)	
3	New Distributor Acquisition	
2	New Customer Acquisition	
2	Launch a New Distributor	
	DAILY TOTAL	

DATE:

APPOINTMENTS

am/pm   am/pm

am/pm   am/pm

am/pm   am/pm

am/pm   am/pm

am/pm   am/pm

am/pm   am/pm

am/pm   am/pm

DAILY NOTES

RECAP YOUR PREVIOUS WEEK

AND

PREPARE FOR YOUR NEXT WEEK

REMEMBER: FULL TIME 50+ POINTS   PART TIME 20+ POINTS

DAILY METHOD OF OPERATION TOTALS FOR THE WEEK

Value	Task	Points
1	Pique Someone's Interest	
1	Successful 3 Way Call	
2	Presentation (1 or 2 guests)	
3	Presentation (3+ guests)	
5	Presentation (5+ guests)	
10	Presentation (10+ guests)	
3	New Distributor Acquisition	
2	New Customer Acquisition	
2	Launch a New Distributor	
	WEEKLY TOTAL	

TOP ACCOMPLISHMENTS FOR THIS PAST WEEK

←

THINGS TO IMPROVE ON

←

GOALS FOR THE COMING WEEK →

IMPORTANT DATES FOR THE COMING WEEK →

MONDAY

TODAY'S TOP PRIORITIES

DAILY METHOD OF OPERATION

Value	Task	Points
1	Pique Someone's Interest	
1	Successful 3 Way Call	
2	Presentation (1 or 2 guests)	
3	Presentation (3+ guests)	
5	Presentation (5+ guests)	
10	Presentation (10+ guests)	
3	New Distributor Acquisition	
2	New Customer Acquisition	
2	Launch a New Distributor	
	DAILY TOTAL	

DATE:

APPOINTMENTS

am/pm   am/pm

am/pm   am/pm

am/pm   am/pm

am/pm   am/pm

am/pm   am/pm

am/pm   am/pm

am/pm   am/pm

DAILY NOTES

TUESDAY

DAILY METHOD OF OPERATION

Value	Task	Points
1	Pique Someone's Interest	
1	Successful 3 Way Call	
2	Presentation (1 or 2 guests)	
3	Presentation (3+ guests)	
5	Presentation (5+ guests)	
10	Presentation (10+ guests)	
3	New Distributor Acquisition	
2	New Customer Acquisition	
2	Launch a New Distributor	
	DAILY TOTAL	

DATE:

APPOINTMENTS

am/pm   am/pm

am/pm   am/pm

am/pm   am/pm

am/pm   am/pm

am/pm   am/pm

am/pm   am/pm

am/pm   am/pm

DAILY NOTES

WEDNESDAY

TODAY'S TOP PRIORITIES

DAILY METHOD OF OPERATION

Value	Task	Points
1	Pique Someone's Interest	
1	Successful 3 Way Call	
2	Presentation (1 or 2 guests)	
3	Presentation (3+ guests)	
5	Presentation (5+ guests)	
10	Presentation (10+ guests)	
3	New Distributor Acquisition	
2	New Customer Acquisition	
2	Launch a New Distributor	
	DAILY TOTAL	

DATE:

APPOINTMENTS

---

am/pm   am/pm

am/pm   am/pm

am/pm   am/pm

am/pm   am/pm

am/pm   am/pm

am/pm   am/pm

am/pm   am/pm

DAILY NOTES

THURSDAY

TODAY'S TOP PRIORITIES

DAILY METHOD OF OPERATION

Value	Task	Points
1	Pique Someone's Interest	
1	Successful 3 Way Call	
2	Presentation (1 or 2 guests)	
3	Presentation (3+ guests)	
5	Presentation (5+ guests)	
10	Presentation (10+ guests)	
3	New Distributor Acquisition	
2	New Customer Acquisition	
2	Launch a New Distributor	
	DAILY TOTAL	

DATE:

APPOINTMENTS

---

am/pm _____   am/pm _____

am/pm _____   am/pm _____

am/pm _____   am/pm _____

am/pm _____   am/pm _____

am/pm _____   am/pm _____

am/pm _____   am/pm _____

am/pm _____   am/pm _____

DAILY NOTES

_____

_____

_____

_____

_____

_____

FRIDAY

TODAY'S TOP PRIORITIES

DAILY METHOD OF OPERATION

Value	Task	Points
1	Pique Someone's Interest	
1	Successful 3 Way Call	
2	Presentation (1 or 2 guests)	
3	Presentation (3+ guests)	
5	Presentation (5+ guests)	
10	Presentation (10+ guests)	
3	New Distributor Acquisition	
2	New Customer Acquisition	
2	Launch a New Distributor	
	DAILY TOTAL	

DATE:

APPOINTMENTS

_____ am/pm _____   _____ am/pm _____

_____ am/pm _____   _____ am/pm _____

_____ am/pm _____   _____ am/pm _____

_____ am/pm _____   _____ am/pm _____

_____ am/pm _____   _____ am/pm _____

_____ am/pm _____   _____ am/pm _____

_____ am/pm _____   _____ am/pm _____

DAILY NOTES

_____

_____

_____

_____

_____

SATURDAY

DAILY METHOD OF OPERATION

Value	Task	Points
1	Pique Someone's Interest	
1	Successful 3 Way Call	
2	Presentation (1 or 2 guests)	
3	Presentation (3+ guests)	
5	Presentation (5+ guests)	
10	Presentation (10+ guests)	
3	New Distributor Acquisition	
2	New Customer Acquisition	
2	Launch a New Distributor	
	DAILY TOTAL	

DATE:

APPOINTMENTS

---

am/pm _____   am/pm _____

am/pm _____   am/pm _____

am/pm _____   am/pm _____

am/pm _____   am/pm _____

am/pm _____   am/pm _____

am/pm _____   am/pm _____

am/pm _____   am/pm _____

DAILY NOTES

_____

_____

_____

_____

_____

_____

SUNDAY

TODAY'S TOP PRIORITIES

DAILY METHOD OF OPERATION

Value	Task	Points
1	Pique Someone's Interest	
1	Successful 3 Way Call	
2	Presentation (1 or 2 guests)	
3	Presentation (3+ guests)	
5	Presentation (5+ guests)	
10	Presentation (10+ guests)	
3	New Distributor Acquisition	
2	New Customer Acquisition	
2	Launch a New Distributor	
	DAILY TOTAL	

DATE:

APPOINTMENTS

---

am/pm _____   am/pm _____

am/pm _____   am/pm _____

am/pm _____   am/pm _____

am/pm _____   am/pm _____

am/pm _____   am/pm _____

am/pm _____   am/pm _____

am/pm _____   am/pm _____

DAILY NOTES

_____

_____

_____

_____

_____

_____

_____

RECAP YOUR PREVIOUS WEEK

AND

PREPARE FOR YOUR NEXT WEEK

REMEMBER: FULL TIME 50+ POINTS   PART TIME 20+ POINTS

DAILY METHOD OF OPERATION TOTALS FOR THE WEEK

Value	Task	Points
1	Pique Someone's Interest	
1	Successful 3 Way Call	
2	Presentation (1 or 2 guests)	
3	Presentation (3+ guests)	
5	Presentation (5+ guests)	
10	Presentation (10+ guests)	
3	New Distributor Acquisition	
2	New Customer Acquisition	
2	Launch a New Distributor	
	WEEKLY TOTAL	

← **TOP ACCOMPLISHMENTS FOR THIS PAST WEEK**

← **THINGS TO IMPROVE ON**

GOALS FOR THE COMING WEEK →

IMPORTANT DATES FOR THE COMING WEEK →

MONDAY

TODAY'S TOP PRIORITIES

DAILY METHOD OF OPERATION

Value	Task	Points
1	Pique Someone's Interest	
1	Successful 3 Way Call	
2	Presentation (1 or 2 guests)	
3	Presentation (3+ guests)	
5	Presentation (5+ guests)	
10	Presentation (10+ guests)	
3	New Distributor Acquisition	
2	New Customer Acquisition	
2	Launch a New Distributor	
	DAILY TOTAL	

DATE:

APPOINTMENTS

---

am/pm _____

am/pm _____

am/pm _____

am/pm _____

am/pm _____

am/pm _____

am/pm _____

am/pm _____

am/pm _____

am/pm _____

am/pm _____

am/pm _____

am/pm _____

am/pm _____

DAILY NOTES

TUESDAY

TODAY'S TOP PRIORITIES

DAILY METHOD OF OPERATION

Value	Task	Points
1	Pique Someone's Interest	
1	Successful 3 Way Call	
2	Presentation (1 or 2 guests)	
3	Presentation (3+ guests)	
5	Presentation (5+ guests)	
10	Presentation (10+ guests)	
3	New Distributor Acquisition	
2	New Customer Acquisition	
2	Launch a New Distributor	
	DAILY TOTAL	

DATE:

APPOINTMENTS

_____ am/pm _____   _____ am/pm _____

_____ am/pm _____   _____ am/pm _____

_____ am/pm _____   _____ am/pm _____

_____ am/pm _____   _____ am/pm _____

_____ am/pm _____   _____ am/pm _____

_____ am/pm _____   _____ am/pm _____

_____ am/pm _____   _____ am/pm _____

DAILY NOTES

WEDNESDAY

TODAY'S TOP PRIORITIES

DAILY METHOD OF OPERATION

Value	Task	Points
1	Pique Someone's Interest	
1	Successful 3 Way Call	
2	Presentation (1 or 2 guests)	
3	Presentation (3+ guests)	
5	Presentation (5+ guests)	
10	Presentation (10+ guests)	
3	New Distributor Acquisition	
2	New Customer Acquisition	
2	Launch a New Distributor	
	DAILY TOTAL	

DATE:

APPOINTMENTS

am/pm   am/pm

am/pm   am/pm

am/pm   am/pm

am/pm   am/pm

am/pm   am/pm

am/pm   am/pm

am/pm   am/pm

DAILY NOTES

THURSDAY

TODAY'S TOP PRIORITIES

DAILY METHOD OF OPERATION

Value	Task	Points
1	Pique Someone's Interest	
1	Successful 3 Way Call	
2	Presentation (1 or 2 guests)	
3	Presentation (3+ guests)	
5	Presentation (5+ guests)	
10	Presentation (10+ guests)	
3	New Distributor Acquisition	
2	New Customer Acquisition	
2	Launch a New Distributor	
	DAILY TOTAL	

DATE:

APPOINTMENTS

am/pm   am/pm

am/pm   am/pm

am/pm   am/pm

am/pm   am/pm

am/pm   am/pm

am/pm   am/pm

am/pm   am/pm

DAILY NOTES

FRIDAY

TODAY'S TOP PRIORITIES

DAILY METHOD OF OPERATION

Value	Task	Points
1	Pique Someone's Interest	
1	Successful 3 Way Call	
2	Presentation (1 or 2 guests)	
3	Presentation (3+ guests)	
5	Presentation (5+ guests)	
10	Presentation (10+ guests)	
3	New Distributor Acquisition	
2	New Customer Acquisition	
2	Launch a New Distributor	
	DAILY TOTAL	

DATE:

APPOINTMENTS

_____ am/pm	_____ am/pm
_____ am/pm	_____ am/pm
_____ am/pm	_____ am/pm
_____ am/pm	_____ am/pm
_____ am/pm	_____ am/pm
_____ am/pm	_____ am/pm
_____ am/pm	_____ am/pm

DAILY NOTES

SATURDAY

DAILY METHOD OF OPERATION

Value	Task	Points
1	Pique Someone's Interest	
1	Successful 3 Way Call	
2	Presentation (1 or 2 guests)	
3	Presentation (3+ guests)	
5	Presentation (5+ guests)	
10	Presentation (10+ guests)	
3	New Distributor Acquisition	
2	New Customer Acquisition	
2	Launch a New Distributor	
	DAILY TOTAL	

DATE:

APPOINTMENTS

am/pm   am/pm

am/pm   am/pm

am/pm   am/pm

am/pm   am/pm

am/pm   am/pm

am/pm   am/pm

am/pm   am/pm

DAILY NOTES

_____

_____

_____

_____

_____

_____

SUNDAY

TODAY'S TOP PRIORITIES

DAILY METHOD OF OPERATION

Value	Task	Points
1	Pique Someone's Interest	
1	Successful 3 Way Call	
2	Presentation (1 or 2 guests)	
3	Presentation (3+ guests)	
5	Presentation (5+ guests)	
10	Presentation (10+ guests)	
3	New Distributor Acquisition	
2	New Customer Acquisition	
2	Launch a New Distributor	
	DAILY TOTAL	

DATE:

APPOINTMENTS

am/pm   am/pm

am/pm   am/pm

am/pm   am/pm

am/pm   am/pm

am/pm   am/pm

am/pm   am/pm

am/pm   am/pm

DAILY NOTES

RECAP YOUR PREVIOUS WEEK

AND

PREPARE FOR YOUR NEXT WEEK

REMEMBER: FULL TIME 50+ POINTS   PART TIME 20+ POINTS

DAILY METHOD OF OPERATION TOTALS FOR THE WEEK

Value	Task	Points
1	Pique Someone's Interest	
1	Successful 3 Way Call	
2	Presentation (1 or 2 guests)	
3	Presentation (3+ guests)	
5	Presentation (5+ guests)	
10	Presentation (10+ guests)	
3	New Distributor Acquisition	
2	New Customer Acquisition	
2	Launch a New Distributor	
	WEEKLY TOTAL	

← TOP ACCOMPLISHMENTS FOR THIS PAST WEEK

← THINGS TO IMPROVE ON

GOALS FOR THE COMING WEEK →

IMPORTANT DATES FOR THE COMING WEEK →

MONDAY

TODAY'S TOP PRIORITIES

DAILY METHOD OF OPERATION

Value	Task	Points
1	Pique Someone's Interest	
1	Successful 3 Way Call	
2	Presentation (1 or 2 guests)	
3	Presentation (3+ guests)	
5	Presentation (5+ guests)	
10	Presentation (10+ guests)	
3	New Distributor Acquisition	
2	New Customer Acquisition	
2	Launch a New Distributor	
	DAILY TOTAL	

DATE:

APPOINTMENTS

am/pm   am/pm

am/pm   am/pm

am/pm   am/pm

am/pm   am/pm

am/pm   am/pm

am/pm   am/pm

am/pm   am/pm

DAILY NOTES

TUESDAY

DAILY METHOD OF OPERATION

Value	Task	Points
1	Pique Someone's Interest	
1	Successful 3 Way Call	
2	Presentation (1 or 2 guests)	
3	Presentation (3+ guests)	
5	Presentation (5+ guests)	
10	Presentation (10+ guests)	
3	New Distributor Acquisition	
2	New Customer Acquisition	
2	Launch a New Distributor	
	DAILY TOTAL	

DATE:

APPOINTMENTS

am/pm   am/pm

am/pm   am/pm

am/pm   am/pm

am/pm   am/pm

am/pm   am/pm

am/pm   am/pm

am/pm   am/pm

DAILY NOTES

WEDNESDAY

TODAY'S TOP PRIORITIES

DAILY METHOD OF OPERATION

Value	Task	Points
1	Pique Someone's Interest	
1	Successful 3 Way Call	
2	Presentation (1 or 2 guests)	
3	Presentation (3+ guests)	
5	Presentation (5+ guests)	
10	Presentation (10+ guests)	
3	New Distributor Acquisition	
2	New Customer Acquisition	
2	Launch a New Distributor	
	DAILY TOTAL	

DATE:

APPOINTMENTS

am/pm   am/pm

am/pm   am/pm

am/pm   am/pm

am/pm   am/pm

am/pm   am/pm

am/pm   am/pm

am/pm   am/pm

DAILY NOTES

THURSDAY

TODAY'S TOP PRIORITIES

DAILY METHOD OF OPERATION

Value	Task	Points
1	Pique Someone's Interest	
1	Successful 3 Way Call	
2	Presentation (1 or 2 guests)	
3	Presentation (3+ guests)	
5	Presentation (5+ guests)	
10	Presentation (10+ guests)	
3	New Distributor Acquisition	
2	New Customer Acquisition	
2	Launch a New Distributor	
	DAILY TOTAL	

DATE:

APPOINTMENTS

am/pm   am/pm

am/pm   am/pm

am/pm   am/pm

am/pm   am/pm

am/pm   am/pm

am/pm   am/pm

am/pm   am/pm

DAILY NOTES

FRIDAY

TODAY'S TOP PRIORITIES

DAILY METHOD OF OPERATION

Value	Task	Points
1	Pique Someone's Interest	
1	Successful 3 Way Call	
2	Presentation (1 or 2 guests)	
3	Presentation (3+ guests)	
5	Presentation (5+ guests)	
10	Presentation (10+ guests)	
3	New Distributor Acquisition	
2	New Customer Acquisition	
2	Launch a New Distributor	
	DAILY TOTAL	

DATE:

APPOINTMENTS

---

am/pm _____   am/pm _____

am/pm _____   am/pm _____

am/pm _____   am/pm _____

am/pm _____   am/pm _____

am/pm _____   am/pm _____

am/pm _____   am/pm _____

am/pm _____   am/pm _____

DAILY NOTES

_____

_____

_____

_____

_____

_____

SATURDAY

DAILY METHOD OF OPERATION

Value	Task	Points
1	Pique Someone's Interest	
1	Successful 3 Way Call	
2	Presentation (1 or 2 guests)	
3	Presentation (3+ guests)	
5	Presentation (5+ guests)	
10	Presentation (10+ guests)	
3	New Distributor Acquisition	
2	New Customer Acquisition	
2	Launch a New Distributor	
	DAILY TOTAL	

DATE:

APPOINTMENTS

am/pm   am/pm

am/pm   am/pm

am/pm   am/pm

am/pm   am/pm

am/pm   am/pm

am/pm   am/pm

am/pm   am/pm

DAILY NOTES

SUNDAY

DAILY METHOD OF OPERATION

Value	Task	Points
1	Pique Someone's Interest	
1	Successful 3 Way Call	
2	Presentation (1 or 2 guests)	
3	Presentation (3+ guests)	
5	Presentation (5+ guests)	
10	Presentation (10+ guests)	
3	New Distributor Acquisition	
2	New Customer Acquisition	
2	Launch a New Distributor	
	DAILY TOTAL	

DATE:

APPOINTMENTS

am/pm   am/pm

am/pm   am/pm

am/pm   am/pm

am/pm   am/pm

am/pm   am/pm

am/pm   am/pm

am/pm   am/pm

DAILY NOTES

RECAP YOUR PREVIOUS WEEK
AND
PREPARE FOR YOUR NEXT WEEK

REMEMBER: FULL TIME 50+ POINTS   PART TIME 20+ POINTS

DAILY METHOD OF OPERATION TOTALS FOR THE WEEK

Value	Task	Points
1	Pique Someone's Interest	
1	Successful 3 Way Call	
2	Presentation (1 or 2 guests)	
3	Presentation (3+ guests)	
5	Presentation (5+ guests)	
10	Presentation (10+ guests)	
3	New Distributor Acquisition	
2	New Customer Acquisition	
2	Launch a New Distributor	
	WEEKLY TOTAL	

← **TOP ACCOMPLISHMENTS FOR THIS PAST WEEK**

← **THINGS TO IMPROVE ON**

➡ **???**

YOU NEED A NEW 90 DAY BLITZ PLANNER

Congratulations on completing your 90 Day Blitz! Now what do you do...?

START ANOTHER 90 DAY BLITZ!

In network marketing, your 90 Day Blitz doesn't necessarily start when you first sign up. It starts when you decide that what you have been doing hasn't been working and you need to focus and set goals to get to where you want to be. This 90 day blitz planner was created by network marketers for network marketers because no matter what company, what product, what service, or whatever your compensation plan is, all network marketers will go through the same things! Because this business is about duplication, you need to duplicate out to your team as fast as you can and by staying guided with a 90 Day Blitz, you will do so efficiently. Thank you for using our planner and we hope you do another blitz and use us again!

Holidays and Observances

2016

JAN 1	New Year's Day	**SEP 5**	Labor Day
JAN 18	Martin Luther King Jr. Day	**OCT 10**	Columbus Day
FEB 14	Valentine's Day	**OCT 31**	Halloween
FEB 15	President's Day	**NOV 8**	Election Day
MAR 27	Easter Sunday	**NOV 11**	Veteran's Day
APR 18	Taxes Due	**NOV 24**	Thanksgiving Day
MAY 8	Mother's Day	**DEC 24**	Christmas Eve
MAY 30	Memorial Day	**DEC 25**	Christmas Day
JUN 19	Father's Day	**DEC 26**	Christmas Day Observed
JUL 4	Independence Day	**DEC 31**	New Year's Eve

2017

JAN 1	New Year's Day	**JUL 4**	Independance Day
JAN 2	New Year's Day Observed	**SEP 4**	Labor Day
JAN 16	Martin Luther King Jr. Day	**OCT 9**	Columbus Day
FEB 14	Valentine's Day	**OCT 31**	Halloween
FEB 20	President's Day	**NOV 11**	Veteran's Day
APR 16	Easter Sunday	**NOV 23**	Thanksgiving Day
APR 18	Taxes Due	**DEC 24**	Christmas Eve
MAY 14	Mother's Day	**DEC 25**	Christmas Day
MAY 29	Memorial Day	**DEC 31**	New Year's Eve
JUN 18	Father's Day		

Holidays and Observances

2018

JAN 1	New Year's Day	**SEP 3**	Labor Day
JAN 15	Martin Luther King Jr. Day	**OCT 8**	Columbus Day
FEB 14	Valentine's Day	**OCT 31**	Halloween
FEB 19	President's Day	**NOV 11**	Veteran's Day
APR 1	Easter Sunday	**NOV 22**	Thanksgiving Day
APR 17	Taxes Due	**DEC 24**	Christmas Eve
MAY 13	Mother's Day	**DEC 25**	Christmas Day
MAY 28	Memorial Day	**DEC 31**	New Year's Eve
JUN 17	Father's Day		
JUL 4	Independance Day		

Thank you for supporting the effort that has gone into making this planner. While there are other products out there in our industry, most are large and expensive or you have to print out yourself and that gets even more expensive (believe us, our old version was $50 USD).

If this planner helped you out, please refer it to your downline as that helps US out and helps your business grow. Make sure to leave a review on Amazon so that other network marketers can benefit from our work!

Again, thank you so much for your support and we wish you the best of luck in this amazing industry!

"Either you run the day or the day runs you."

- Jim Rohn, American author

Jim Rohn. (n.d.). BrainyQuote.com. Retrieved December 1, 2016, from BrainyQuote.com
Web site: https://www.brainyquote.com/quotes/quotes/j/jimrohn162051.html

Made in the USA
Columbia, SC
06 October 2017